7/14

DISCARD

Andrew Luck

by Josh Gregory

Consultant: Barry Wilner
AP Football Writer

BEARPORT
PUBLISHING

New York, New York

Publisher: Kenn Goin
Senior Editor: Joyce Tavolacci
Creative Director: Spencer Brinker
Photo Researcher: Josh Gregory
Design: Emily Love

Library of Congress Cataloging-in-Publication Data

Gregory, Josh.
  Andrew Luck / by Josh Gregory.
      pages cm. — (Football stars up close)
  Includes bibliographical references and index.
  ISBN 978-1-62724-084-0 (library binding) — ISBN 1-62724-084-5 (library binding)
 1. Luck, Andrew, 1989—Juvenile literature. 2. Football players—United States—Juvenile literature. I. Title.
  GV939.L81G74 2014
  796.332092—dc23
  [B]
                            2013032723

For more information, write to Bearport Publishing Company, Inc., 45 West 21st Street, Suite 3B, New York, New York 10010. Printed in the United States of America.

10 9 8 7 6 5 4 3 2 1

Contents

Running Out of Time

It was the start of the 2012–2013 **NFL** season. The Indianapolis Colts were playing against the Minnesota Vikings. The score was tied 20–20 with just 31 seconds left in the game. Colts **quarterback** Andrew Luck needed to score before time ran out. The pressure was on. He threw two 20-yard (18 m) passes. The Colts were now 40 yards (37 m) from the **end zone**. Could Andrew help his team win the game?

Andrew (#12) begins a play against the Minnesota Vikings.

Andrew (left) gained an average of 7.2 yards (6.6 m) per play in the game against the Vikings.

Andrew was only 23 years old when his team battled the Vikings in 2012.

The First Win

On the next play, Andrew pretended to call for a **snap**. He tricked the Vikings into moving **offside**. This **penalty** allowed the Colts to move five yards (4.6 m) closer to the end zone. Because of Andrew's smart play, the team could try for a **field goal**. Andrew's teammate, Adam Vinatieri, kicked the ball. It sailed through the goalposts. Score! Andrew's quick thinking had helped lead to his first win in the NFL.

Andrew celebrating after the Vikings' game

The Colts' win against the Vikings was only Andrew's second game as an NFL player.

Andrew threw two touchdown passes during the 2012 Colts-Vikings game.

A Football Family

Andrew has loved football ever since he was a child. He was born on September 12, 1989, in Washington, D.C. Andrew's father, Oliver Luck, had been a quarterback for the Houston Oilers. Later, his father managed football teams. As a result, Andrew spent his childhood going to lots of games. When he was 12 years old, Andrew began playing quarterback in a football league.

Andrew shares a love of football with his father, Oliver Luck.

Oliver Luck about to make a pass

Oliver Luck was quarterback for the Houston Oilers from 1983 to 1986.

High School Star

In his youth football league, Andrew's speed, strength, and smarts helped him stand out. When he started high school, Andrew soon became a star player. He was great at throwing long passes and avoiding tackles. As a result, **scouts** from top colleges began closely watching him.

Andrew has worn the number 12 since he was in high school.

Andrew was a star player for the Stratford High School football team in Houston.

In high school, Andrew was a great student who graduated at the top of his class.

Colleges Come Calling

Many colleges wanted Andrew to join their team. Andrew picked Stanford University in California. It is one of the best schools in the country. He wanted to get a good education, as well as play football. However, the school's football team wasn't very good. It would take a lot of hard work to help turn the team around. Andrew was ready for the challenge.

Stanford University

Andrew playing for
Stanford University

Stanford's football team
is called the Cardinal.

Super Start

In his second year of college, Andrew became Stanford's **starting** quarterback. The team soon began to win more games. Over the next three years, Andrew helped lead Stanford to three **bowl games**. He became known for his precise passing and speed. Andrew won many awards for his expert plays. He was even a **finalist** for the Heisman Trophy two times!

The Heisman Trophy is an award given each year to the best player in college football.

Andrew (center) threw 82 touchdown passes during his last three seasons at Stanford.

In 2011, Andrew won the Johnny Unitas Golden Arm Award, which is given to the nation's top college quarterback.

Draft Days

In 2011, many NFL teams wanted Andrew to leave Stanford and play for them. He would have been one of the first players picked in the **draft**. However, Andrew chose to finish his last year of college. He joined the NFL draft in 2012. The Indianapolis Colts chose Andrew as the very first pick! "I felt on top of the world," remembers Andrew.

In 2011, the Colts tied with the St. Louis Rams for the worst record in the NFL. As a result, the Colts received first pick in the 2012 draft.

Colts fans welcome Andrew to the team.

The Colts selected
Andrew over 252
other college players
in the 2012 NFL draft.

Rising Star

Andrew had a big role to fill in Indianapolis. During the prior season, the Colts had won only 2 out of 16 games. Andrew was ready to help turn things around. During his **rookie** season, he led the Colts to 11 wins. He ran and passed the football for a total gain of 4,629 yards (4,233 m). This was more than any other rookie quarterback in NFL history!

Andrew practiced hard to prepare for his first season in the NFL.

Andrew threw 23 touchdown passes during the 2012–2013 regular season.

Andrew about to fire off a pass

A Bright Future

The Colts' great 2012–2013 season led them to the **playoffs**. Andrew guided his team in a tough game against the Baltimore Ravens. The Colts played well, but they lost 24–9. Andrew didn't make it to the **Super Bowl** that year. Yet he had done something incredible. He had led the Colts from having the worst record in the NFL all the way to making the playoffs!

Andrew (#12) threw for 288 yards (263 m) against the Ravens, but it wasn't enough to win the game.

Andrew takes the field
during a Colts game.

In 2012, Andrew worked with
Indiana University to start a
program that teaches kids about
health and fitness.

Andrew's Life and Career

★ **September 12, 1989** Andrew Luck is born in Washington, D.C.

★ **2001** Andrew begins playing in a youth football league.

★ **2004** Andrew begins high school.

★ **2008** Andrew begins college at Stanford University.

★ **2009** Andrew becomes the starting quarterback for Stanford's football team.

★ **2010–2011** Andrew is runner-up for the Heisman Trophy both years.

★ **2011** Andrew leads the Stanford Cardinal against the Virginia Tech Hokies in the Orange Bowl.

★ **2012** Andrew is chosen as the first overall pick in the NFL draft by the Indianapolis Colts.

★ **2013** Andrew leads the Indianapolis Colts against the Baltimore Ravens in the first round of the playoffs.

Glossary

bowl games (BOHL GAYMZ) games that are played after the regular college football season ends

draft (DRAFT) an event in which professional football teams take turns choosing college athletes to play for them

end zone (END ZOHN) the area at either end of a football field where touchdowns are scored

field goal (FEELD GOHL) a score of three points made by kicking the ball through the other team's goalposts

finalist (FYE-nuh-list) someone who has reached the last part of a competition

NFL (EN-EFF-ELL) letters standing for the National Football League, which includes 32 teams

offside (AWF-side) when a player has broken the rules of the game by moving forward, ahead of the ball

penalty (PEN-uhl-tee) a punishment for a football team that breaks the rules

playoffs (PLAY-awfss) the games held after the regular football season that determine which two teams will compete in the Super Bowl

quarterback (KWOR-tur-bak) a football player who leads the offense, the part of the team that moves the ball forward

rookie (RUK-ee) a player in his or her first season in a sport

scouts (SKOUTS) football experts who search for talented young players to join their team

snap (SNAP) the action in which a football is handed to the quarterback, beginning a play

starting (START-ing) being the coach's first choice to play in a game

Super Bowl (SOO-pur BOHL) the final championship game of the NFL season

Index

Bibliography

Official Site of the Indianapolis Colts: www.colts.com

Official Site of the NFL: www.nfl.com

Read More

Kelley, K. C. *Indianapolis Colts (Favorite Football Teams).* Mankato, MN:
 Child's World (2010).

MacRae, Sloan. *The Indianapolis Colts (America's Greatest Teams).*
 New York: PowerKids Press (2011).

Peloza, Brian. *Indianapolis Colts (Inside the NFL).* Edina, MN: ABDO
 (2011).

Sandler, Michael. *Peyton Manning and the Indianapolis Colts: Super
 Bowl XLI (Super Bowl Superstars).* New York: Bearport (2008).

Learn More Online

To learn more about Andrew Luck, visit
www.bearportpublishing.com/FootballStarsUpClose